SONGS FROM Disney Moana

COLLECTION FOR YOUNG VOICES

T0081795

TABLE OF CONTENTS

Characters and Artwork © Disney Enterprises, Inc.

Walt Disney Music Company
Wonderland Music Company, Inc.

DISTRIBUTED BY

7777 W. BLUEMOUND RD. P.O. BOX 13819 MILWAUKEE, WI 53213

In Australia Contact:
Hal Leonard Australia Pty. Ltd.
4 Lentara Court
Cheltenham, Victoria, 3192 Australia
Email: ausadmin@halleonard.com.au

Visit Hal Leonard Online at
www.halleonard.com

HOW FAR I'LL GO

Music and Lyrics by
LIN-MANUEL MIRANDA

turn I take, ev-'ry trail I track, ev-'ry path I make, ev-'ry road leads back to the
place I know where I can-not go, where I long____ to be. See the

15 A bit quicker (♩ = 84)

opt. harmony in lower notes

line where the sky meets the sea, it calls____ me, and no one
knows____ how far it goes.____ If the

wind in my sail on the sea stays be-hind___ me, one day I'll

know.___ If I go, there's just no tell-ing how far I'll

go. I___ know___ ev-'ry-bod-y on this is-land___ seems___ so hap-py on this

is - land.___ Ev-'ry-thing is by de-sign.___

I know ev - 'ry - bod - y on this is - land_ has_ a role on this

is - land,_ so may-be I can roll with mine._ I can

lead with pride, I can make us strong. I'll be sat - is - fied if I play a - long, but the

voice in - side sings a dif - f'rent song. What is wrong with me?

See the light as it shines on the sea: it's blind -

- ing, but no one knows_____ how deep it goes._____ And it

seems like it's call-ing out to me, so come find_____ me and let me

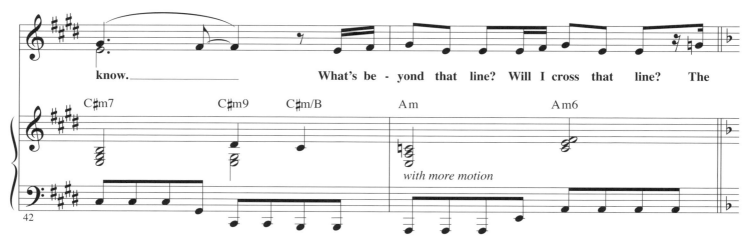

know._____ What's be - yond that line? Will I cross that line? The

line where the sky meets the sea, it calls___ me,_____ and no one

knows___ how far it goes.___ If the

wind in my sail on the sea stays be - hind___ me, one day I'll

know___ how far I'll go!___

SHINY

Music by LIN-MANUEL MIRANDA
and MARK MANCINA
Lyrics by LIN-MANUEL MIRANDA

shin - y! Send your ar - mies, but they'll nev - er be e - nough: my shell's too tough, Mau - i, man.

Well, you could try, try, try, but you can't ex - pect a dem - i - god to beat a dec - a - pod. Look it up.

You will die, die, die: now it's time for me to take a - part your ach - ing heart.

Far from _ the ones who _ a - ban - doned _ you, chas - ing _ the

shin - y. Now I eat you, so pre - pare your fi - nal plea, just for me. You'll

nev - er be quite as shin - y; you wish you were nice and shin - y. _____

WE KNOW THE WAY

Music by OPETAIA FOA'I
Lyrics by OPETAIA FOA'I and
LIN-MANUEL MIRANDA

*Tay fay-noo-ah tay mah-lee yay. Nah-yay koh hah-kee-lee-yah

WHERE YOU ARE

Music by LIN-MANUEL MIRANDA,
OPETAIA FOA'I and MARK MANCINA
Lyrics by LIN-MANUEL MIRANDA

Moderately fast (♩ = 112)

a - na! Make way! Make way!___ Mo-a - na, it's time you knew

the vil - lage of Mo - tu - nui is all you need.___

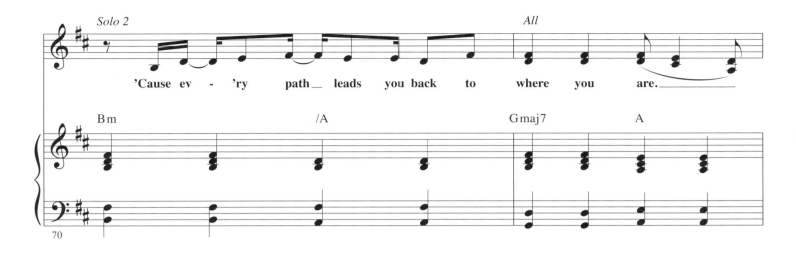

Solo 2 .... *All*

'Cause ev - 'ry path___ leads you back to where you are.___

Bm   /A   Gmaj7   A

70

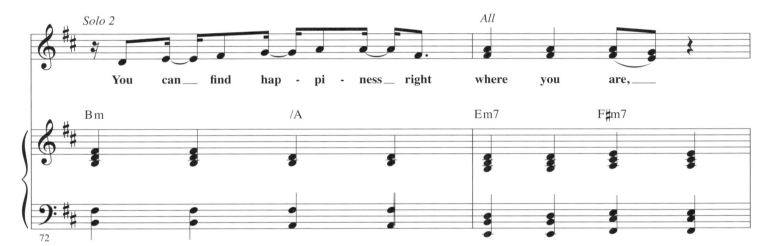

Solo 2 .... *All*

You can___ find hap - pi - ness___ right where you are,___

Bm   /A   Em7   F♯m7

72

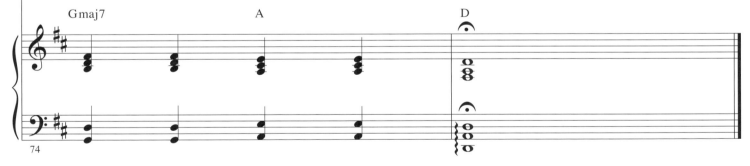

where you are.___

Gmaj7   A   D

74

YOU'RE WELCOME

Music and Lyrics by
LIN-MANUEL MIRANDA

-come. Huh! I guess it's just my way of be-ing me! ____ You're wel-

Bb   **D**   **D7**   **Gm**

49

opt. Solo

-come! You're wel - come! Well, come to think of it:

Eb   **Bb**   **Bb5**

52

55 *mf*

Kid, hon-est-ly, I could go on and on. I could ex-plain ev-'ry nat-ur-al phe-nom-e-non.

Bb5

mf

55

The tide? The grass? The ground? Oh that was Mau-i just mess-ing a-round.

57

I killed an eel. I bur-ied its guts. Sprout-ed a tree now you got co-co-nuts.

What's the les - son? What is the take - a - way? Don't mess with Mau - i when he's on a break - a - way,

D♭5   D5   F♯5

and the tap - es - try here in my skin is a map of the vic - t'ries I win!

Gm   E♭

Look where I've been, I make ev - 'ry-thing hap - pen! Look at that mean min - i - Mau - i just tick - e - ty

B♭   D